LATIN'S NOT SO TOUGH!

LEVEL ONE

A Classical Latin Worktext
by
Karen Mohs

Dear Parent/Teacher:

Welcome to the exciting world of Classical Latin!

This Level One workbook allows the child to learn by doing. Each lesson builds on the previous lesson. Therefore, a systematic approach is recommended.

Daily drill will assist memory and assure success in this study. You may remove the flashcard pages at the end of the workbook, cut out the letters, and copy, paste, or tape them onto 3 by 5 inch cards.

Begin use of flashcards after the first workbook page. As the child learns each new letter, diphthong, or special consonant, add it to the flashcard stack. Check the box at the bottom of each page to record and encourage consistency.

An answer key is available, as well as quizzes/exams, flashcards on a ring, and an audio pronunciation CD or cassette tape.

References for this series include *First Year Latin* by Charles Jenney, Jr., *Second Year Latin* by Charles Jenney, Jr., and *The New College Latin & English Dictionary* by John C. Traupman, Ph.D.

Enjoy learning Latin!

ISBN 1-931842-50-7

Greek 'n' Stuff
P.O. Box 882
Moline, IL 61266-0882
www.greeknstuff.com

Revised 9/04

This workbook
belongs to me:

_____

(student's name)

because
I'M LEARNING LATIN!

TABLE OF CONTENTS

Latin Workbook - Level 1
Copyright © 1996 by Karen Mohs

Ā* ā

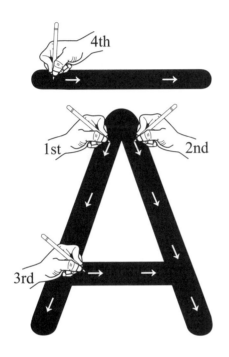

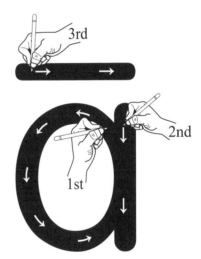

Write the letters across each line.
As you write them, say the sound of "**a**" in *father*.

Ā

ā

*The short line above certain Latin vowels is called a *macron*.

Circle the words that have the ā sound.

mark   quaint

calm   jacket

nail   darn

garden   battle

ham   hurrah

pale   salsa

A a

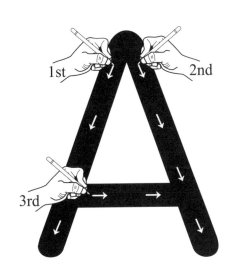 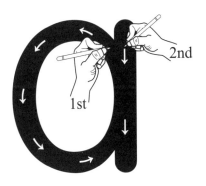

Write the letters across each line.
As you write them, say the sound of **"a"** in *idea*.

A — — — — — — — — — — — — — — — — — — —

a — — — — — — — — — — — — — — — — — — —

You now know two letters of the Latin alphabet. Start your
flashcard deck with these letters and practice them every day.
(See back of workbook for flashcards.)

☐ I practiced my flashcards today.

REMEMBER!
A or ɑ sounds like **a** in *idea*.

Draw a line from the letter to its sound.

ɑ   **a** in *father*

ā   **a** in *idea*

Circle the words that have the ɑ sound.

canoe   far

arch   alike

math   ravine

soda   ace

☐   I practiced my flashcards today.

4

B b

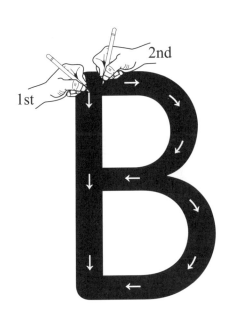

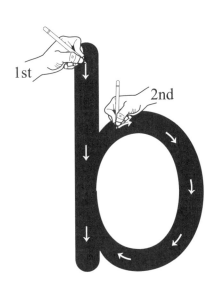

Write the letters across each line.
As you write them, say the sound of "**b**" in *boy*.

B

b

☐ I practiced my flashcards today.
(Remember to add this new card to your flashcards.)

REMEMBER!
B or b sounds like **b** in ***boy***.

Circle the words that have the sound at the beginning of the row.

ā	cat star haste jar rash father
a	gag bat wait along afar salad
b	box bed kick cook sprain bat
ā	safe tank scarf far sparkle pack
a	arise along jam plate drag away

☐ I practiced my flashcards today.

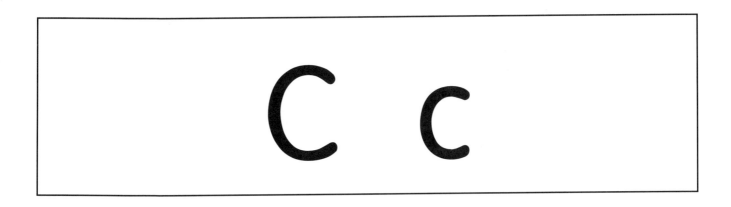

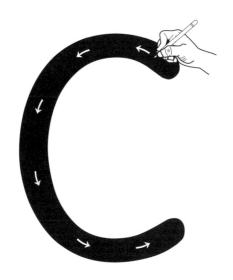
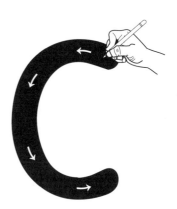

Write the letters across each line.
As you write them, say the sound of "**c**" in *cat*.

C

c

☐ I practiced my flashcards today.
(Remember to add this new card to your flashcards.)

Draw a line from the Latin letter to its sound.

ā   **b** in *boy*

b   **c** in *cat*

a   **a** in *father*

c   **a** in *idea*

Circle the words that have the Latin c sound.

city

cane   cedar

cat   cell

come

cup   cost

center

cinder   cub

coat   cent

☐ I practiced my flashcards today.

Latin Workbook - Level 1
Copyright © 1996 by Karen Mohs

D d

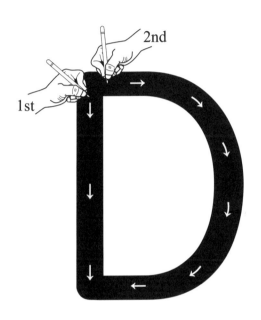 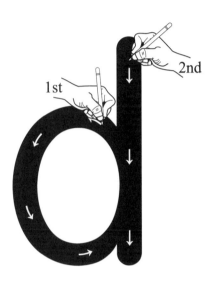

Write the letters across each line.
As you write them, say the sound of "**d**" in ***dog***.

D

d

☐ I practiced my flashcards today.
(Remember to add this new card to your flashcards.)

Circle *yes* if the sentence is true. Circle *no* if it is not true.

yes *no* 1. The Latin letter b sounds like the **b** in *boy*.

yes *no* 2. The Latin letter ā sounds like the **a** in *cape*.

yes *no* 3. The Latin letter c sounds like the **c** in *cent*.

yes *no* 4. The Latin letter ā sounds like the **a** in *father*.

yes *no* 5. The Latin letter a sounds like the **a** in *sat*.

yes *no* 6. The Latin letter d sounds like the **d** in *dog*.

☐ I practiced my flashcards today.

Ē ē

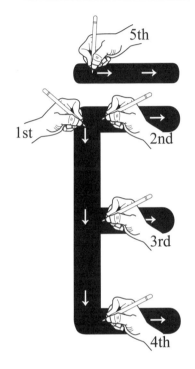

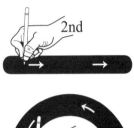

Write the letters across each line.
As you write them, say the sound of **"ey"** in *obey*.

Ē

ē

☐ I practiced my flashcards today.
(Remember to add this new card to your flashcards.)

> # REMEMBER!
> Ē or ē sounds like **ey** in *obey*.

Fill in the blanks with the missing lowercase Latin letters.

1. Latin _____ sounds like the **b** in *boy*.

2. Latin _____ sounds like the **ey** in *obey*.

3. Latin _____ sounds like the **c** in *cat*.

4. Latin _____ sounds like the **a** in *father*.

5. Latin _____ sounds like the **a** in *idea*.

6. Latin _____ sounds like the **d** in *dog*.

☐ I practiced my flashcards today.

E e

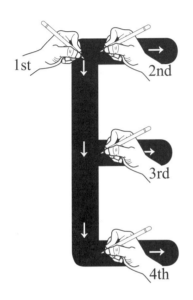

Write the letters across each line.
As you write them, say the sound of "**e**" in *bet*.

E -

e _____

☐ I practiced my flashcards today.
(Remember to add this new card to your flashcards.)

REMEMBER!
E or e sounds like **e** in *bet*.

Write the words under the correct Latin sounds.

get	wet	stay	bless
brake	step	weigh	grace

ē   e

_____   _____

- - - - - - - - - - - - -   - - - - - - - - - - - - -

_____   _____

- - - - - - - - - - - - -   - - - - - - - - - - - - -

_____   _____

- - - - - - - - - - - - -   - - - - - - - - - - - - -

_____   _____

- - - - - - - - - - - - -   - - - - - - - - - - - - -

_____   _____

- - - - - - - - - - - - -   - - - - - - - - - - - - -

_____   _____

☐ I practiced my flashcards today.

Latin Workbook - Level 1
Copyright © 1996 by Karen Mohs

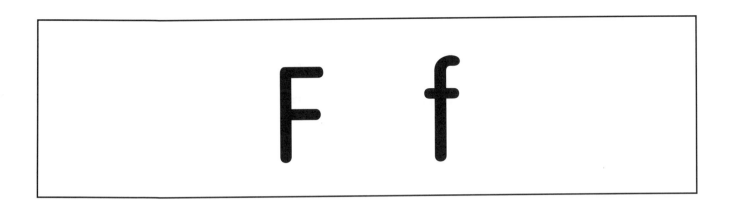

F f

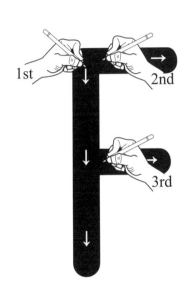

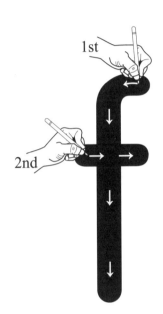

Write the letters across each line.
As you write them, say the sound of **"f"** in *fan*.

F -

f -

☐ I practiced my flashcards today.
(Remember to add this new card to your flashcards.)

REMEMBER!
F or f sounds like **f** in *fan*.

Match the Latin letters with their sounds.

c   **a** in *father*

f   **e** in *get*

e   **c** in *cat*

ā   **f** in *fan*

b   **b** in *boy*

ē   **d** in *dog*

a   **ey** in *obey*

d   **a** in *idea*

☐   I practiced my flashcards today.

G g

 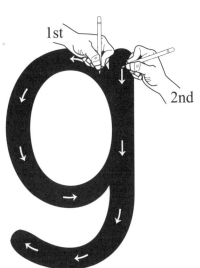

Write the letters across each line.
As you write them, say the sound of "**g**" in *go*.

G

g

REMEMBER!
G or g sounds like **g** in *go*.

Look at the Latin letter in the corner of the box.
Circle the words that have the sound it makes.

e	wet deep head thread reap	c	cash percent cease catch cable
f	very fact even fish fever	ē	may key wave eye braid
g	ginger fig geese age gray	d	dust red day baby map

☐ I practiced my flashcards today.

18

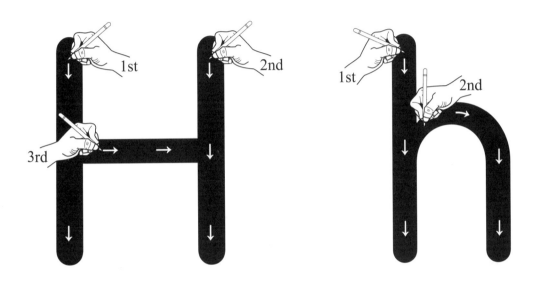

Write the letters across each line.
As you write them, say the sound of "**h**" in *hat*.

H

h

REMEMBER!
H or h sounds like **h** in *hat*.

Circle the letters that match the sound in the big box.

g in *go*	b	b	g	c
	g	c	b	g
h in *hat*	h	g	h	b
	a	d	b	h
ey in *obey*	e	ā	e	ē
	a	ē	ā	e
e in *get*	i	ē	e	ē
	e	a	e	a
f in *fan*	f	t	f	l
	l	f	l	t

☐ I practiced my flashcards today.

Latin Workbook - Level 1
Copyright © 1996 by Karen Mohs

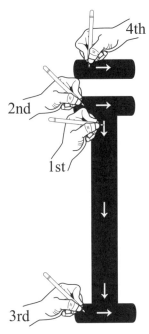

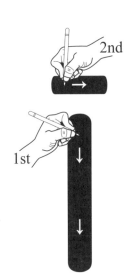

Write the letters across each line.
As you write them, say the sound of "**i**" in *machine*.

REMEMBER!
Ī or ī sounds like **i** in *machine*.

Fill in the blanks with the missing lowercase Latin letters.

$\overline{}$

1. Latin _____ sounds like the **h** in *hat*.

$\overline{}$

2. Latin _____ sounds like the **f** in *fan*.

$\overline{}$

3. Latin _____ sounds like the **ey** in *obey*.

$\overline{}$

4. Latin _____ sounds like the **g** in *go*.

$\overline{}$

5. Latin _____ sounds like the **i** in *machine*.

$\overline{}$

6. Latin _____ sounds like the **e** in *get*.

☐ I practiced my flashcards today.

Latin Workbook - Level 1
Copyright © 1996 by Karen Mohs

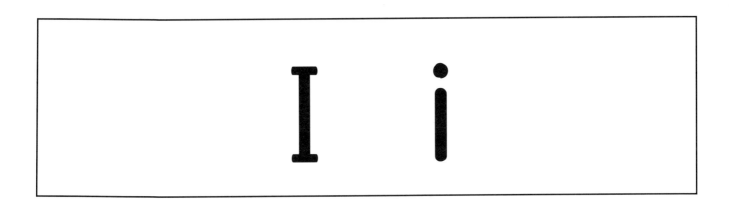

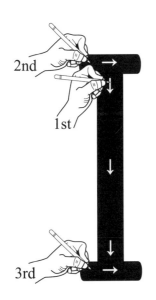

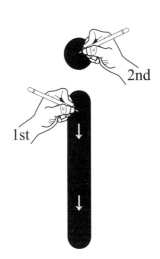

Write the letters across each line.
As you write them, say the sound of "**i**" in *sit*.

I

i

☐ I practiced my flashcards today.
(Remember to add this new card to your flashcards.)

REMEMBER!
I or i sounds like **i** in *sit*.

Write the words under the correct Latin sounds.

green	street	miss	mean
sip	bit	free	grin

ī

i

☐ I practiced my flashcards today.

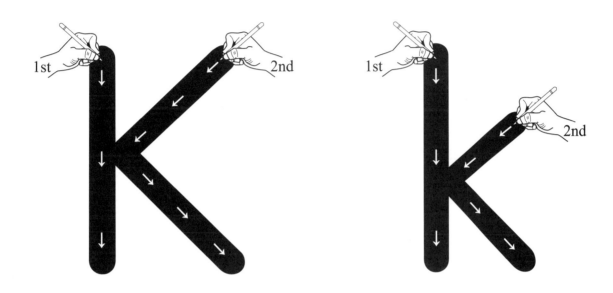

Write the letters across each line.
As you write them, say the sound of "**k**" in *king*.

K -

k -

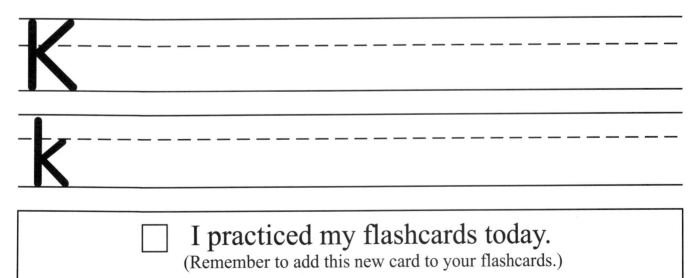

☐ I practiced my flashcards today.
(Remember to add this new card to your flashcards.)

REMEMBER!
K or k sounds like **k** in *king*.

Circle the words that have the sound of the Latin letter at the beginning of the row.

i	sit	shut	dish
k	slice	kiss	king
b	hood	boy	baby
c	cook	cat	rice
ā	crane	barn	father
g	go	give	gem
ē	seat	ray	obey
ī	bean	light	machine
f	cave	fan	food
h	him	hat	this
e	get	ate	west

☐ I practiced my flashcards today.

Latin Workbook - Level 1
Copyright © 1996 by Karen Mohs

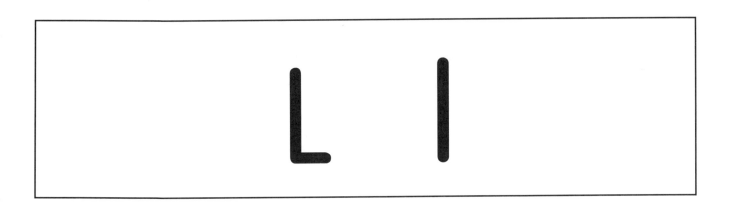

Write the letters across each line.
As you write them, say the sound of "**l**" in *land*.

L

l

REMEMBER!
L or l sounds like **l** in *land*.

Color the triangle if the Latin letter matches the sound.

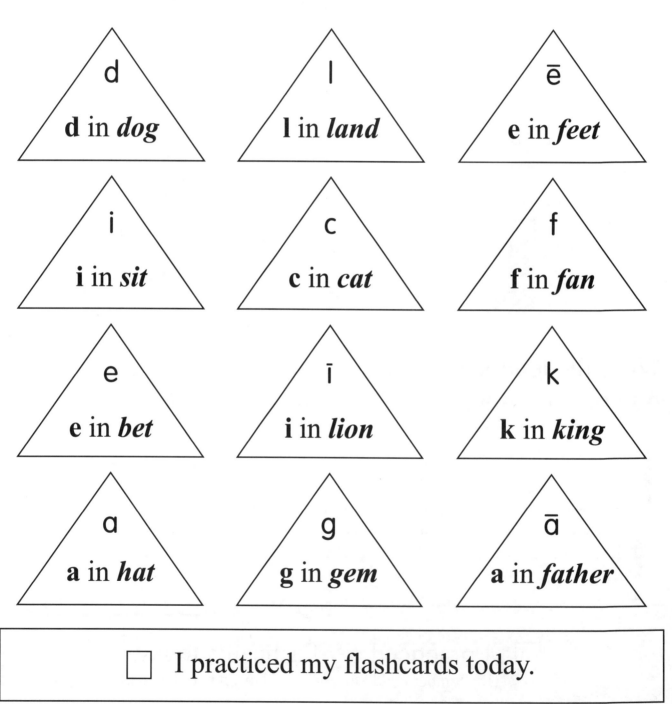

M m

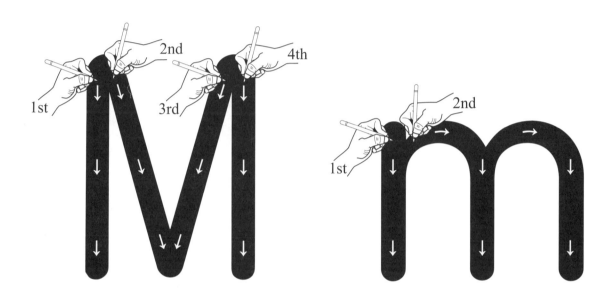

Write the letters across each line.
As you write them, say the sound of **"m"** in *man*.

M

m

☐ I practiced my flashcards today.
(Remember to add this new card to your flashcards.)

Put a *circle* on the words that have the Latin a sound.*
Put a *box* on the words that have the Latin e sound.
Put a *triangle* on the words that have the Latin i sound.

bite   slept   hay   trip

    away
                        soda   bee

            rake
leg   ten   thing

    camel   get
                        sat   game

                        tip
list   tight   cat
                                    giant

                            reap
    angel   miss

        wet
meet   way   sad

*Careful! It may not be the English "a" that makes the Latin "a" sound.

☐ I practiced my flashcards today.

N n

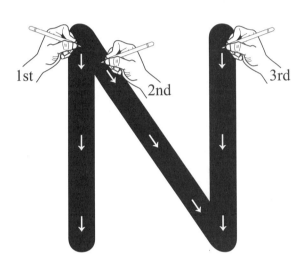 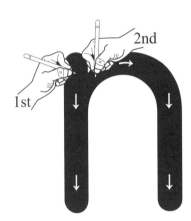

Write the letters across each line.
As you write them, say the sound of **"n"** in *nut*.

N —

n —

☐ I practiced my flashcards today.
(Remember to add this new card to your flashcards.)

REMEMBER!
N or n sounds like **n** in *nut*.

Match the Latin letters with their sounds.

i	**l** in *land*
l	**i** in *sit*
n	**i** in *machine*
g	**n** in *nut*
h	**h** in *hat*
ī	**k** in *king*
m	**g** in *go*
k	**m** in *man*

☐ I practiced my flashcards today.

Ō ō

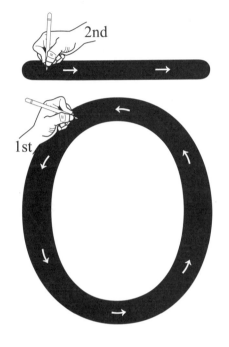

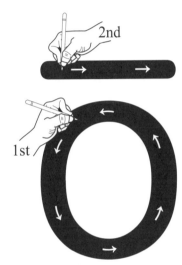

Write the letters across each line.
As you write them, say the sound of "**o**" in ***note***.

Ō —

ō —

☐ I practiced my flashcards today.
(Remember to add this new card to your flashcards.)

REMEMBER!
Ō or ō sounds like **o** in *note*.

Fill in the blanks with the missing lowercase Latin letters.

_____
- - - - - -

1. Latin _____ sounds like the **m** in *man*.

_____
- - - - - -

2. Latin _____ sounds like the **k** in *king*.

_____
- - - - - -

3. Latin _____ sounds like the **i** in *sit*.

_____
- - - - - -

4. Latin _____ sounds like the **l** in *land*.

_____
- - - - - -

5. Latin _____ sounds like the **o** in *note*.

_____
- - - - - -

6. Latin _____ sounds like the **n** in *nut*.

☐ I practiced my flashcards today.

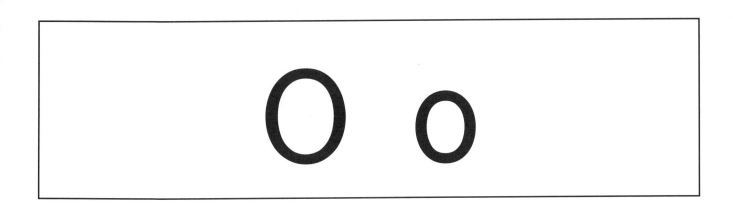

Write the letters across each line.
As you write them, say the sound of "**o**" in *omit*.

O -

o -

☐ I practiced my flashcards today.
(Remember to add this new card to your flashcards.)

Write the words under the correct Latin sounds.

obey	bone	omit	float
omega	bowl	roast	okay

Ō	o

*Both Latin "o" sounds are "long." The ō as in *note* is held longer than the o as in *omit*.

P p

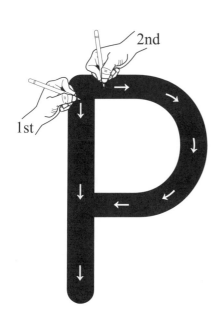 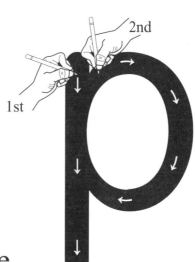

Write the letters across each line.
As you write them, say the sound of "**p**" in *pit*.

P –

p –

☐ I practiced my flashcards today.
(Remember to add this new card to your flashcards.)

Circle *yes* if the sentence is true. Circle *no* if it is not true.

yes *no* 1. The Latin letter m sounds like the **m** in *mice*.

yes *no* 2. The Latin letter ρ sounds like the **p** in *pan*.

yes *no* 3. The Latin letter o sounds like the **o** in *hot*.

yes *no* 4. The Latin letter c sounds like the **c** in *ocean*.

yes *no* 5. The Latin letter n sounds like the **n** in *napkin*.

yes *no* 6. The Latin letter ō sounds like the **o** in *rob*.

☐ I practiced my flashcards today.

Latin Workbook - Level 1
Copyright © 1996 by Karen Mohs

Q q

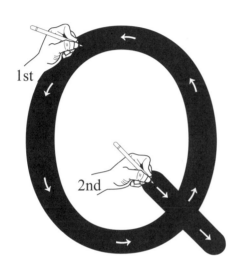

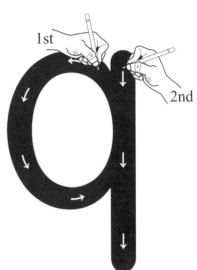

Write the letters across each line.
As you write them, say the sound of **"qu"** in *quit*.

Qu

qu

☐ **I practiced my flashcards today.**
(Remember to add this new card to your flashcards.)

REMEMBER!
Qu or qu sounds like **qu** in *quit*.

Draw a stem from each flower to its vase.

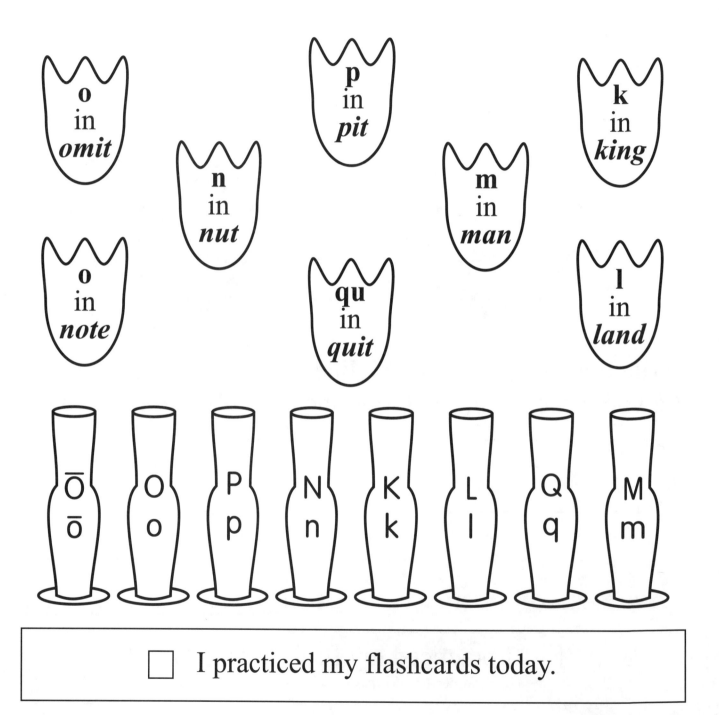

☐ I practiced my flashcards today.

R r

 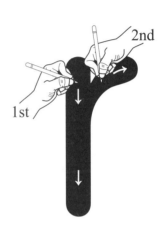

Write the letters across each line.
As you write them, say the sound of **"r"** in ***run***.

R –

r –

☐ I practiced my flashcards today.
(Remember to add this new card to your flashcards.)

REMEMBER!
R or r sounds like **r** in *run*.

Circle the correct Latin letter below each sound.

o in *note*		i in *machine*		m in *man*	
ō	o	ī	i	n	m
ey in *obey*		**c in *cat***		**e in *bet***	
ē	e	c	q	ē	e
r in *run*		**a in *father***		**p in *pit***	
v	r	ā	a	p	q
n in *nut*		**qu in *quit***		**k in *king***	
n	m	c	qu	k	qu
o in *omit*		**i in *sit***		**a in *idea***	
ō	o	ī	i	ā	a

☐ I practiced my flashcards today.

S s

Write the letters across each line.
As you write them, say the sound of "**s**" in *sit*.

S -

s -

☐ I practiced my flashcards today.
(Remember to add this new card to your flashcards.)

Look at the Latin letter in the corner of the box.
Circle the words that have the sound it makes.

o	vote okay Ohio boot omit	s	easy century tease sash salt
c	cable face cattle cream race	ō	hope mop grow cone root
r	when five argue barrel rat	ē	eye table day baby eat

☐ I practiced my flashcards today.

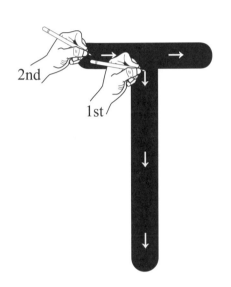

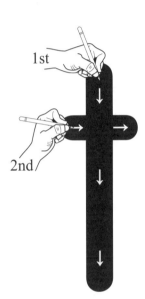

Write the letters across each line.
As you write them, say the sound of "**t**" in *tag*.

T

t

☐ I practiced my flashcards today.
(Remember to add this new card to your flashcards.)

Circle the words that have the sound of the Latin letters at the beginning of the row.

s	can sat	days yes	less fuse
t	tag the	mat treat	thank thing
ō	fox roam	toast often	omit bold
p	graph phone	pie apple	scrap rack
o	obey okay	goat hog	frog oasis

☐ I practiced my flashcards today.

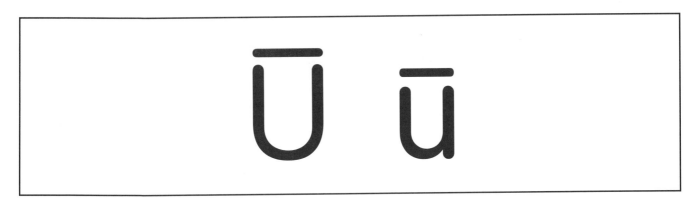

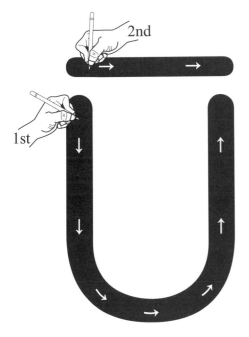

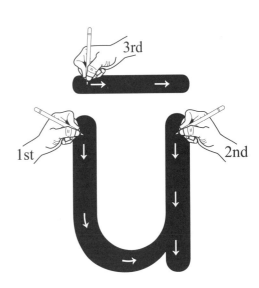

Write the letters across each line.
As you write them, say the sound of "**u**" in *rule*.

Ū --

ū --

☐ **I practiced my flashcards today.**
(Remember to add this new card to your flashcards.)

REMEMBER!
Ū or ū sounds like **u** in *rule*.

Fill in the blanks with the missing lowercase Latin letters.

1. Latin _____ sounds like the **p** in *pit*.

2. Latin _____ sounds like the **s** in *sit*.

3. Latin _____ sounds like the **t** in *tag*.

4. Latin _____ sounds like the **qu** in *quit*.

5. Latin _____ sounds like the **u** in *rule*.

6. Latin _____ sounds like the **r** in *run*.

☐ I practiced my flashcards today.

U u

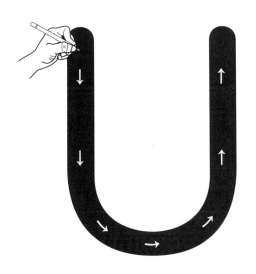 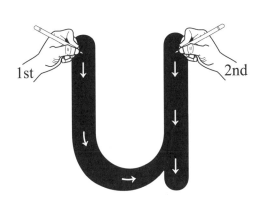

Write the letters across each line.
As you write them, say the sound of "**u**" in *put*.

U

u

REMEMBER!
U or u sounds like **u** in *put*.

Write the words under the correct Latin sounds.

took	book	bloom	drool
boot	glue	lure	full

ū

_____

- - - - - - - - - - - - - - - - -

_____

_____

- - - - - - - - - - - - - - - - -

_____

_____

- - - - - - - - - - - - - - - - -

_____

_____

- - - - - - - - - - - - - - - - -

_____

u

_____

- - - - - - - - - - - - - - - - -

_____

_____

- - - - - - - - - - - - - - - - -

_____

_____

- - - - - - - - - - - - - - - - -

_____

_____

- - - - - - - - - - - - - - - - -

_____

☐ I practiced my flashcards today.

Latin Workbook - Level 1
Copyright © 1996 by Karen Mohs

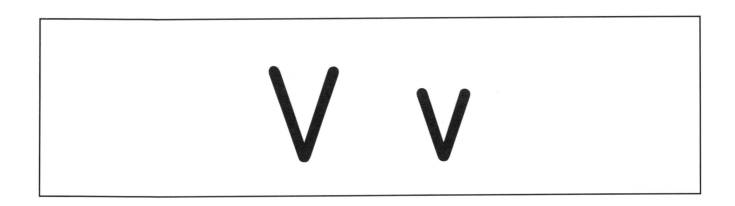

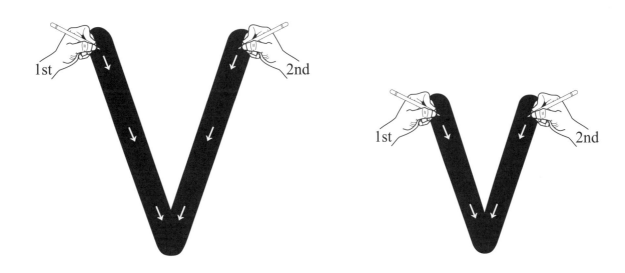

Write the letters across each line.
As you write them, say the sound of "**w**" in ***way***.

V

v

☐ I practiced my flashcards today.
(Remember to add this new card to your flashcards.)

Match the Latin letters with their sounds.

s	**r** in *run*
o	**u** in *rule*
r	**o** in *omit*
ū	**s** in *sit*
v	**o** in *note*
t	**w** in *way*
u	**t** in *tag*
ō	**u** in *put*

☐ I practiced my flashcards today.

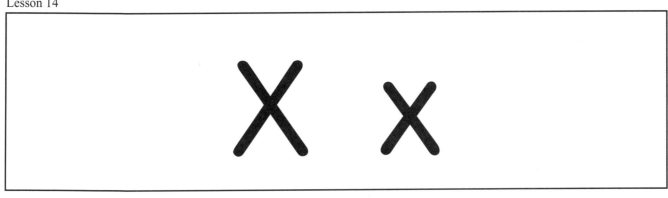

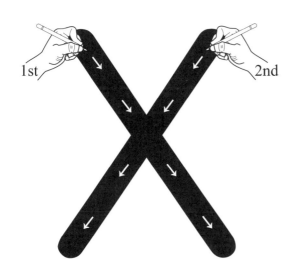

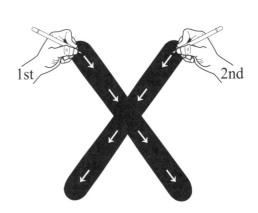

Write the letters across each line.
As you write them, say the sound of **"ks"** in *socks*.

X

X

☐ **I practiced my flashcards today.**
(Remember to add this new card to your flashcards.)

Write the Latin letters for the first sound you hear in the English words.

art   _____   lamb   _____

head   _____   quick   _____

page   _____   sing   _____

win   _____   gag   _____

far   _____   nest   _____

ride   _____   kite   _____

map   _____   table   _____

☐ I practiced my flashcards today.

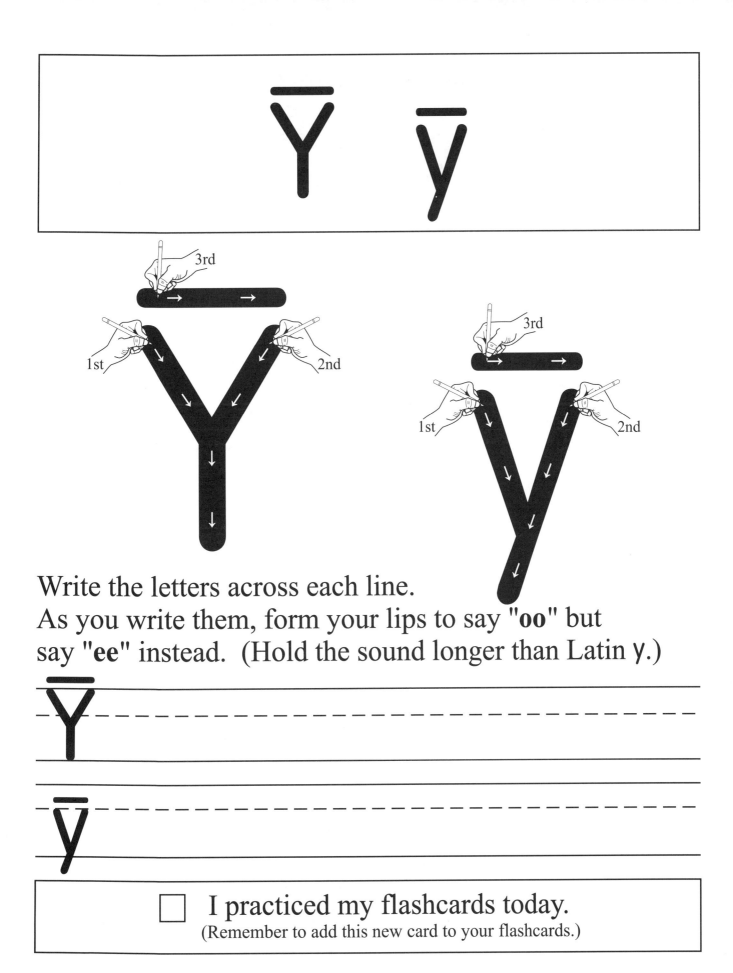

Write the letters across each line.
As you write them, form your lips to say **"oo"** but say **"ee"** instead. (Hold the sound longer than Latin ȳ.)

Ȳ

ȳ

☐ I practiced my flashcards today.
(Remember to add this new card to your flashcards.)

Fill in the blanks with the missing lowercase Latin letters.

_____

_ _ _ _ _ _

1. Latin _____ sounds like the **t** in *tag*.

_____

_ _ _ _ _ _

2. Latin _____ sounds like the **ks** in *socks*.

_____

_ _ _ _ _ _

3. Latin _____ sounds like the **s** in *sit*.

_____

_ _ _ _ _ _

4. Latin _____ sounds like the **w** in *way*.

_____

_ _ _ _ _ _

5. Latin _____ sound is made by forming your
_____ lips to say **oo** but saying **ee** instead.

_ _ _ _ _ _

6. Latin _____ sounds like the **r** in *run*.

☐ I practiced my flashcards today.

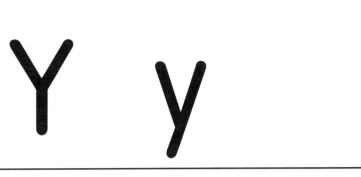

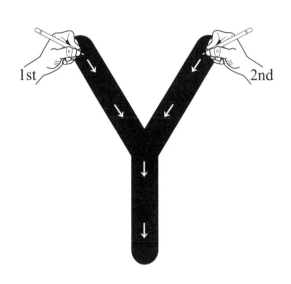

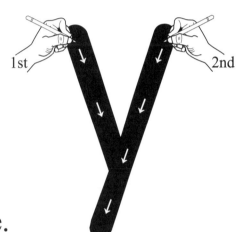

Write the letters across each line.
As you write them, form your lips to say **"oo"** but say **"ee"** instead. (Hold the sound shorter than Latin ȳ.)

Y –

y –

☐ I practiced my flashcards today.
(Remember to add this new card to your flashcards.)

REMEMBER!
The Y or y sound is made when you
form your lips to say **oo** but say **ee** instead.
(Hold it shorter than Latin ȳ.)

Circle *yes* if the sentence is true. Circle *no* if it is not
true.

yes *no* 1. The Latin letter s sounds like the **s** in *has*.

yes *no* 2. The Latin sound for ȳ is held longer than
the Latin sound for y.

yes *no* 3. The Latin letter v sounds like the **v** in *very*.

yes *no* 4. The Latin letter g sounds like the **g** in *age*.

yes *no* 5. The Latin letter c sounds like the **c** in *ace*.

yes *no* 6. The Latin letter e sounds like the **e** in *bee*.

☐ I practiced my flashcards today.

Z z

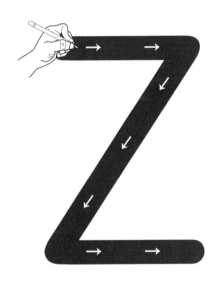 

Write the letters across each line.
As you write them, say the sound of **"dz"** in *adze*.

Z

z

☐ I practiced my flashcards today.
(Remember to add this new card to your flashcards.)

REMEMBER!
Z or z sounds like **dz** in *adze*.

Circle the letters that match the sound in the big box.

u in *put*	ū	u	y
s in *sit*	s	c	z
p in *pit*	p	f	ph
dz in *adze*	k	x	z
o in *note*	ō	o	h
u in *rule*	ū	u	y
o in *omit*	ō	o	h
ks in *socks*	s	k	x
t in *tag*	th	f	t
w in *way*	v	r	u

☐ I practiced my flashcards today.

Latin Workbook - Level 1
Copyright © 1996 by Karen Mohs

LET'S PRACTICE

Circle the words that have the sound of the letter in the big box.

v	wash	west	van
	weed	vast	ever
s	his	same	bus
	miss	busy	kids
ō	hope	rock	over
	bottle	foam	pot
g	God	gentle	gem
	age	gas	get
u	look	shout	pull
	hump	stool	cookie

☐ I practiced my flashcards today.

LET'S PRACTICE

Fill in the blanks with the missing sounds and words.

1. Latin v sounds like the _____ in _____.

2. Latin x sounds like the _____ in _____.

3. Latin u sounds like the _____ in _____.

4. Latin t sounds like the _____ in _____.

5. Latin z sounds like the _____ in _____.

6. Latin ū sounds like the _____ in _____.

☐ I practiced my flashcards today.

DIPHTHONGS

Latin has six diphthongs.

A diphthong combines two vowels to make one sound.

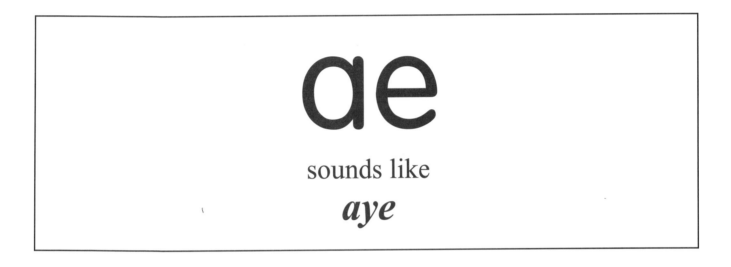

ae

sounds like

aye

Write the diphthong ae across each line.
As you write it, say the "*aye*" sound.

ae

ae

☐ I practiced my flashcards today.
(Remember to add this new card to your flashcards.)

REMEMBER!
ae sounds like *aye*.

Draw a line from the ae in the circle to the words with the Latin ae sound.

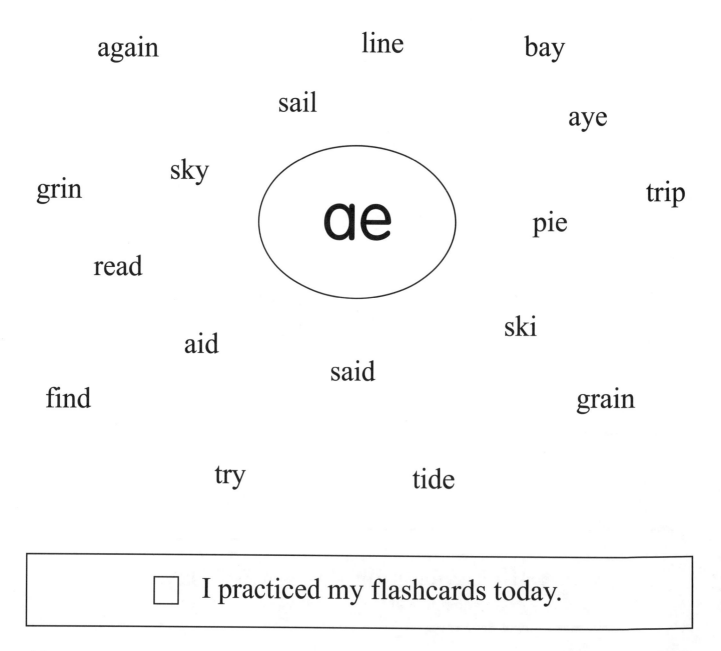

again

line

bay

sail

aye

sky

grin

trip

ae

pie

read

ski

aid

said

find

grain

try

tide

I practiced my flashcards today.

DIPHTHONGS

Write the diphthong that makes the *"aye"* sound.

_____

_ _ _ _ _ _ _ _ _ _ _ _ _ _ _ _ _ _ _

_____

au

sounds like
ow in *now*

Write the diphthong au across each line.
As you write it, say the **"ow"** sound in *now*.

au

au

☐ I practiced my flashcards today.
(Remember to add this new card to your flashcards.)

REMEMBER!
au sounds like **ow** in *now*.

Circle the word with the Latin sound.

ā	nap mane ark	s	has miss busy	o	often obey bone
g	age game engine	ē	blade set reed	au	know cow blow
ae	try say race	c	cent cast grace	i	bit high wide
z	zoo adze zero	v	want save vast	ū	bun rude mule

☐ I practiced my flashcards today.

66

DIPHTHONGS

Draw a line from each diphthong to its sound.

au   *aye*

ae   **ow** in *now*

sounds like
ei in *neighbor*

Write the diphthong ei across each line.
As you write it, say the "**ei**" sound in *neighbor*.

ei –

ei –

☐ I practiced my flashcards today.
(Remember to add this new card to your flashcards.)

REMEMBER!
ei sounds like **ei** in *neighbor*.

Circle the correct Latin letter below each sound.

n in *nut*		**ks** in *socks*		**ei** in *neighbor*	
ȳ	n	x	k	ae	ei
w in *way*		**m** in *man*		**o** in *note*	
v	r	m	n	ō	o
r in *run*		**dz** in *adze*		**p** in *pit*	
t	r	x	z	p	q
aye		**u** in *put*		**s** in *sit*	
ae	ei	ū	u	s	c
t in *tag*		**qu** in *quit*		**ow** in *now*	
g	t	c	qu	au	av

☐ I practiced my flashcards today.

DIPHTHONGS

Circle the correct diphthong for each sound.

ei in *neighbor*	au	ae	ei
ow in *now*	au	ae	ei
aye	au	ae	ei

eu

sounds like

ay-oo (in one syllable)

Write the diphthong eu across each line.
As you write it, say "*ay-oo*" as one syllable.

eu

eu

☐ I practiced my flashcards today.
(Remember to add this new card to your flashcards.)

Write the Latin letters that make the sound on each button.

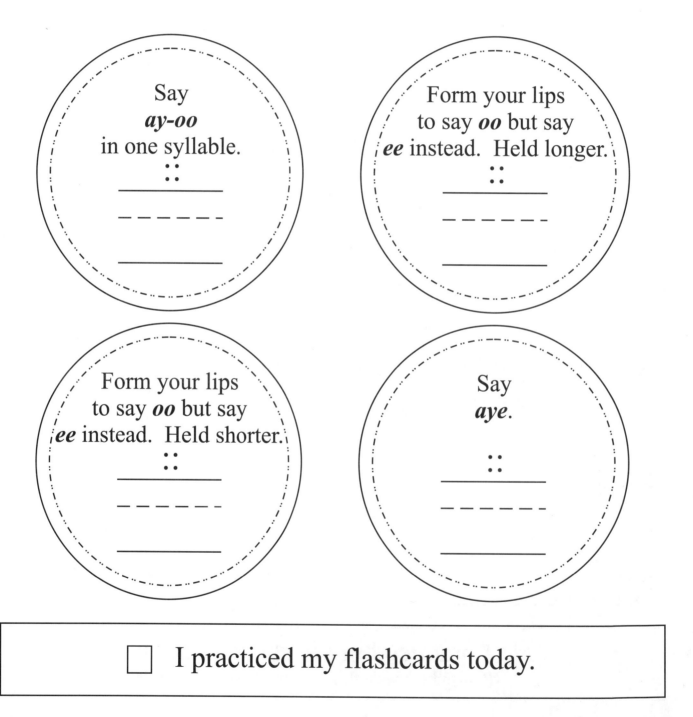

Say
ay-oo
in one syllable.

Form your lips
to say *oo* but say
ee instead. Held longer.

Form your lips
to say *oo* but say
ee instead. Held shorter.

Say
aye.

☐ I practiced my flashcards today.

DIPHTHONGS

Write the correct diphthong for each sound.

_ay-oo_ _____   **ei** in _**neighbor**_ _____

oe

sounds like
oy in _**joy**_

Write the diphthong oe across each line.
As you write it, say the "**oy**" sound in _**joy**_.

oe

oe

☐ I practiced my flashcards today.
(Remember to add this new card to your flashcards.)

REMEMBER!
oe sounds like **oy** in *joy*.

Circle *yes* if the sentence is true. Circle *no* if it is not true.

yes *no* 1. The Latin letters ei sound like the **ei** in *eight*.

yes *no* 2. The Latin letters oe sound like the **oe** in *poet*.

yes *no* 3. The Latin letters au sound like the **ow** in *know*.

yes *no* 4. The Latin letters ae sound like the **ea** in *head*.

yes *no* 5. The Latin letters oe sound like the **oy** in *boy*.

yes *no* 6. The Latin letters eu sound like *ay-oo*.

☐ I practiced my flashcards today.

DIPHTHONGS

Draw a line from each diphthong to its sound.

ay-oo	oe
oy in *joy*	au
ow in *now*	eu

---

ui

sounds like

uee in *queen*

Write the diphthong ui across each line.
As you write it, say the "**uee**" sound in *queen*.

ui -

ui -

☐ I practiced my flashcards today.
(Remember to add this new card to your flashcards.)

Circle the words that have the sound of the Latin letters at the beginning of the row.

oe	toy every	tray boy	enjoy grow
ui	queen equip	weep suit	ruin sweep
ae	guy head	say eat	fly kite
ei	weigh eight	either leaf	rein receive
au	below flow	clown cloud	flower glow

☐ I practiced my flashcards today.

Latin Workbook - Level 1
Copyright © 1996 by Karen Mohs

LET'S PRACTICE

Circle the letters that match the sound in the big box.

ow in *now*	ae	au	ei
	eu	oe	ui
aye	ae	au	ei
	eu	oe	ui
oy in *joy*	ae	au	ei
	eu	oe	ui
uee in *queen*	ae	au	ei
	eu	oe	ui
ay-oo	ae	au	ei
	eu	oe	ui

☐ I practiced my flashcards today.

LET'S PRACTICE

Fill in the blanks with the missing sounds and words.

1. Latin ui sounds like _____ in _____.

2. Latin eu sounds like _____.

3. Latin oe sounds like _____ in _____.

4. Latin au sounds like _____ in _____.

5. Latin ei sounds like _____ in _____.

6. Latin ae sounds like _____.

☐ I practiced my flashcards today.

SPECIAL CONSONANTS

Most Latin consonants sound like the same English consonants, but some have special sounds.

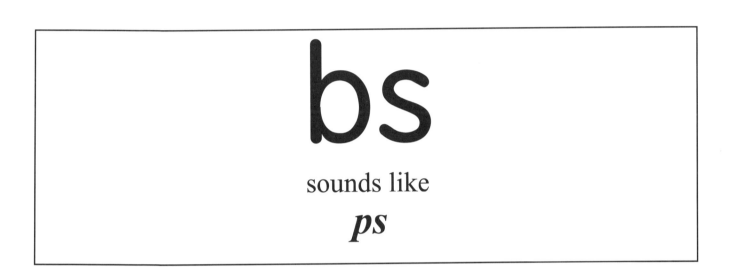

bs

sounds like

ps

Write the consonants bs across each line.
As you write them, say the "***ps***" sound.

bs

bs

☐ I practiced my flashcards today.
(Remember to add this new card to your flashcards.)

Circle the words that have the sound of the Latin letters at the beginning of the row.

s	his	cross	soup
oe	royal	sow	may
ei	side	pie	reign
v	want	vote	wish
ū	shoot	room	plum
ae	day	have	lie
bs	ads	lips	slabs
au	saw	claw	down
g	gust	ago	gem
ui	quiz	queen	weed
u	push	trust	butch

☐ I practiced my flashcards today.

SPECIAL CONSONANTS

Write the Latin consonants that make the "*ps*" sound.

- - - - - - - - - - - - - - - - - -

----

bt

sounds like

pt

Write the consonants bt across each line.
As you write them, say the "*pt*" sound.

bt -

bt -

☐ I practiced my flashcards today.
(Remember to add this new card to your flashcards.)

REMEMBER!
bt sounds like *pt*.

Circle the letters that match the sound in the big box.

ay-oo	ui	ue	eu
ks in *socks*	s	x	k
uee in *queen*	ui	eu	ee
w in *way*	v	r	y
ei in *neighbor*	oa	ie	ei
sounds like *pt*	dt	bt	tb
ow in *now*	au	ov	av
aye	ai	ae	ei
sounds like *ps*	sp	ps	bs
oy in *joy*	eo	oe	eu

☐ I practiced my flashcards today.

SPECIAL CONSONANTS

Draw a line from the special consonants to their sounds.

bt   *pt*

bs   *ps*

ch

sounds like

ch in *character*

Write the consonants ch across each line.
As you write them, say the "**ch**" sound in *character*.

ch

ch

☐ I practiced my flashcards today.
(Remember to add this new card to your flashcards.)

Circle the word with the Latin sound.

c	brace cane rice	**oe**	toe poet boil	**e**	net feet thing
bs	hips absent cabs	**ae**	greed slide bay	**g**	stage gem guess
v	vat ever wing	**ui**	quest tweed build	**ch**	arc chart arch
bt	debt apt table	**au**	toe low loud	**ei**	tie seige vein

☐ I practiced my flashcards today.

Latin Workbook - Level 1
Copyright © 1996 by Karen Mohs

SPECIAL CONSONANTS

Circle the correct special consonants for each sound.

ch	bs	bt	ch
pt	bs	bt	ch
ps	bs	bt	ch

gu

sounds like

gu in *anguish*

Write the consonants gu across each line.
As you write them, say the "**gu**" sound in *anguish*.

gu

gu

☐ I practiced my flashcards today.
(Remember to add this new card to your flashcards.)

Write the Latin letters for the first sound you hear in the English words.

sag	_____	weep
wish	_____	tuck
Guam	_____	omit
owl	_____	aye
nick	_____	mat
eight	_____	rush
pear	_____	oil

☐ I practiced my flashcards today.

Latin Workbook - Level 1
Copyright © 1996 by Karen Mohs

SPECIAL CONSONANTS

Write the special consonants for each sound.

_____   _____
- - - - - - - -   - - - - - - - -

pt _____   *ps* _____

i

sounds like
y in *youth*

Write the consonant **i** across each line.
As you write it, say the "**y**" sound in *youth*.

i -

i -

☐ I practiced my flashcards today.
(Remember to add this new card to your flashcards.)

Fill in the blanks with the missing lowercase Latin letters.

_____
_ _ _ _ _ _
1. Latin _____ sounds like the **gu** in *anguish*.

_____
_ _ _ _ _ _
2. Latin _____ has the *pt* sound.

_____
_ _ _ _ _ _
3. Latin _____ sounds like the **ch** in *character*.

_____
_ _ _ _ _ _
4. Latin _____ sounds like the **uee** in *queen*.

_____
_ _ _ _ _ _
5. Latin _____ , used as a consonant, sounds like
_____ the **y** in *youth*.

_ _ _ _ _ _
6. Latin _____ has the *ps* sound.

☐ I practiced my flashcards today.

SPECIAL CONSONANTS

Draw a line from each special consonant to its sound.

gu in *anguish*   gu

y in *youth*   ch

ch in *character*   i

ph

sounds like

ph in *phone*

Write the consonants ph across each line.
As you write them, say the "**ph**" sound in *phone*.

ph ‑

ph ‑

☐ I practiced my flashcards today.
(Remember to add this new card to your flashcards.)

REMEMBER!
ph sounds like **ph** in *phone*.

Draw a stem from each flower to its vase.

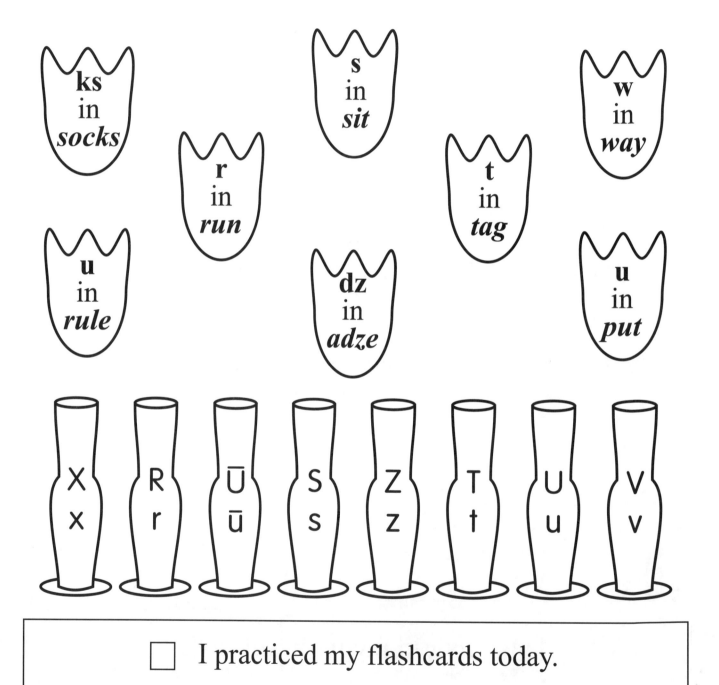

SPECIAL CONSONANTS

Circle the special consonants for each sound.

ps	bs	bt	ph
ph	bs	bt	ph
pt	bs	bt	ph

su

sounds like

su in *suave*

Write the letters su across each line.
As you write them, say the "**su**" sound in *suave*.

su

su

☐ I practiced my flashcards today.
(Remember to add this new card to your flashcards.)

REMEMBER!
su sounds like **su** in *suave*.

Write the Latin letters that make the sound on each pie.

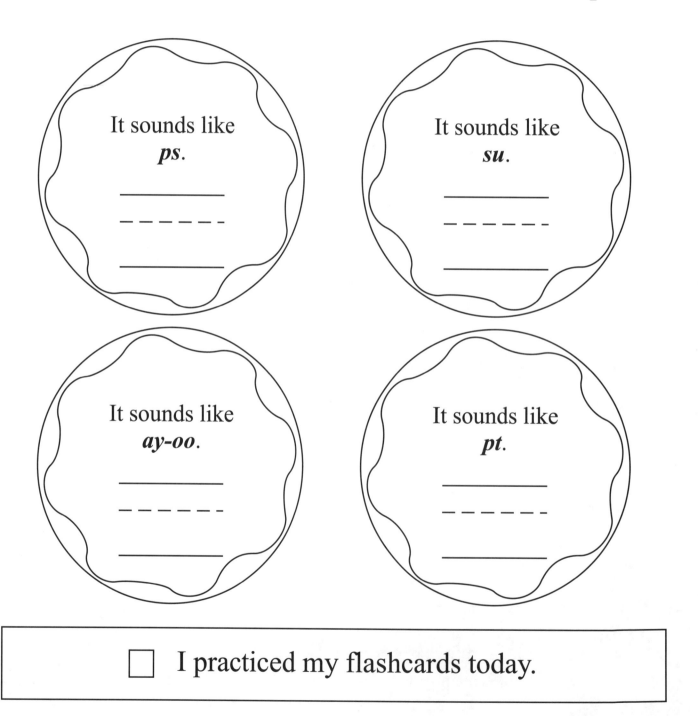

It sounds like
ps.

_____

- - - - - -

_____

It sounds like
su.

_____

- - - - - -

_____

It sounds like
ay-oo.

_____

- - - - - -

_____

It sounds like
pt.

_____

- - - - - -

_____

☐ I practiced my flashcards today.

SPECIAL CONSONANTS

Draw a line from the special consonants to their sounds.

ph in *phone*   i

su in *suave*   su

y in *youth*   ph

sounds like

th in *thick*

Write the consonants th across each line.
As you write them, say the "**th**" sound in *thick*.

th -

th -

☐ I practiced my flashcards today.
(Remember to add this new card to your flashcards.)

REMEMBER!
th sounds like **th** in *thick*.

Draw a line from each kite to its roll of string.

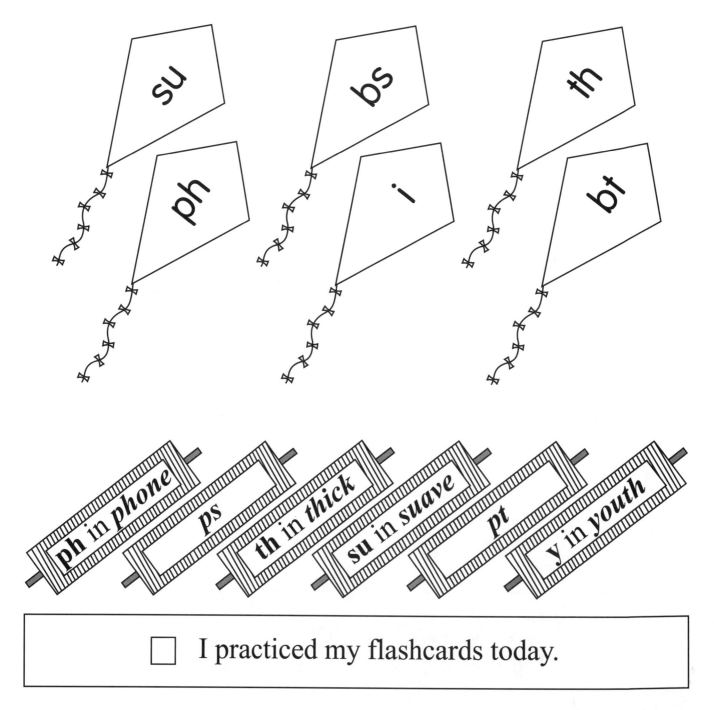

LET'S PRACTICE

Match the Latin letters with their sounds.

gu   **th** in *thick*

ui   **gu** in *anguish*

th   **ph** in *phone*

ei   **uee** in *queen*

ph   **ei** in *neighbor*

ch   **su** in *suave*

i   **oy** in *joy*

su   **ch** in *character*

oe   **y** in *youth*

☐ I practiced my flashcards today.

LET'S PRACTICE

Color the triangle if the Latin letters match the sound.

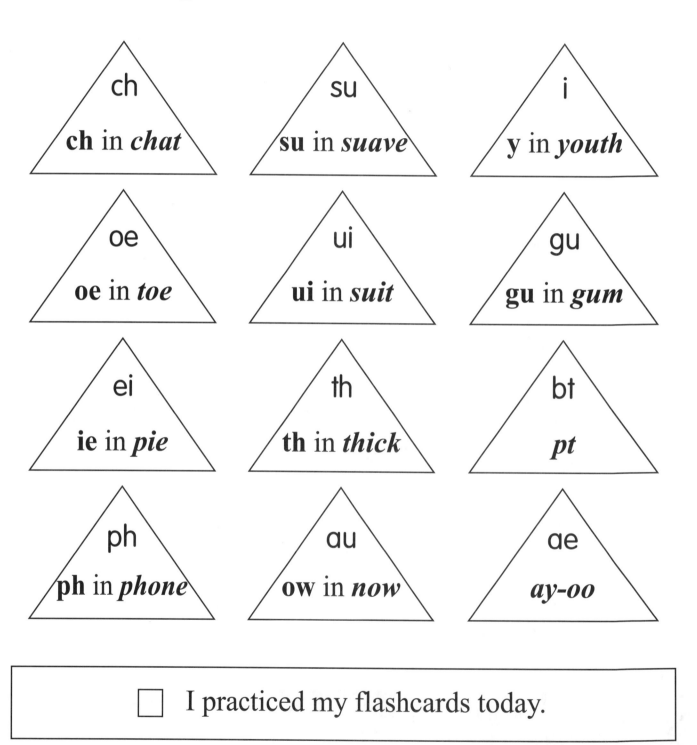

ch

ch in *chat*

su

su in *suave*

i

y in *youth*

oe

oe in *toe*

ui

ui in *suit*

gu

gu in *gum*

ei

ie in *pie*

th

th in *thick*

bt

pt

ph

ph in *phone*

au

ow in *now*

ae

ay-oo

☐ I practiced my flashcards today.

LET'S PRACTICE

Draw a line from each pickle to its jar.

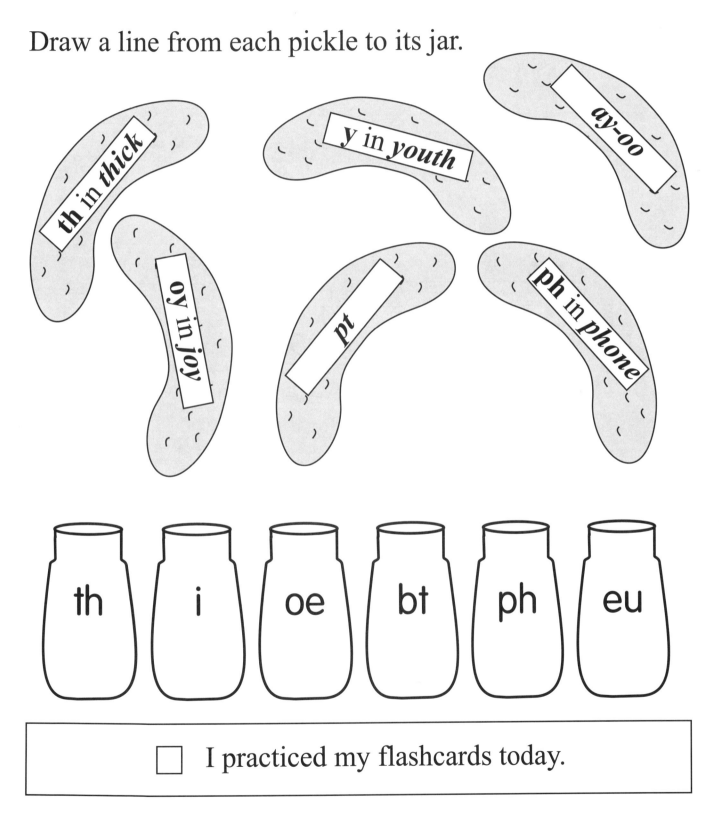

I practiced my flashcards today.

LET'S PRACTICE

Look at the Latin letters in the corner of the box.
Circle the words that have the sound they make.

oe	sew toe boy enjoy coin	**su**	swim sun sue swan sweep
ch	chess ache chrome arch anchor	**bs**	lips caps ribs tubs tops
th	thimble throne this that thank	**ei**	eight receive weird stay rain

☐ I practiced my flashcards today.

LET'S PRACTICE

Fill in the blanks with the missing lowercase Latin letters.

1. Latin _____ sounds like the **su** in *suave*.

2. Latin _____ sounds like the **gu** in *anguish*.

3. Latin _____ sounds like the **ei** in *neighbor*.

4. Latin _____ sounds like the **th** in *thick*.

5. Latin _____ sounds like the **ph** in *phone*.

6. Latin _____ sounds like the **ch** in *character*.

☐ I practiced my flashcards today.

LET'S PRACTICE

Circle the correct Latin letters below each sound.

ks in *socks*		**w** in *way*		**u** in *put*	
kz	x	v	u	ū	u
uee in *queen*		**oy** in *joy*		*ps*	
ui	ē	oy	oe	ps	bs
pt		**y** in *youth*		*ay-oo*	
pt	bt	y	i	eu	ao
aye		**ow** in *now*		**ei** in *neighbor*	
ae	ay	ov	au	ā	ei
c in *cat*		**i** in *machine*		**o** in *note*	
c	s	ī	i	ō	o

☐ I practiced my flashcards today.

LET'S PRACTICE

Circle the letters that match the sound in the big box.

ay-oo	eu	ae	ei
e in *bet*	e	eu	ē
o in *omit*	oe	ō	o
c in *cat*	k	c	ch
y in *youth*	y	i	ȳ
u in *rule*	u	ū	y
pt	pt	ps	bt
i in *machine*	i	ī	y
a in *father*	a	ā	ae
ps	bs	ps	sp

□ I practiced my flashcards today.

LET'S PRACTICE

Circle *yes* if the sentence is true. Circle *no* if it is not true.

yes *no* 1. The Latin letters ch sound like the **ch** in *character*.

yes *no* 2. The Latin letters ui sound like the **ui** in *suit*.

yes *no* 3. The Latin letters th sound like the **th** in *them*.

yes *no* 4. The Latin letters oe sound like the **oy** in *joy*.

yes *no* 5. The Latin letters gu sound like the **gu** in *anguish*.

yes *no* 6. The Latin consonant i sounds like the **y** in *youth*.

yes *no* 7. The Latin letters bs sound like *ps.*

☐ I practiced my flashcards today.

LET'S PRACTICE

Write the Latin letters for the first sound you hear in the English words.

young   _____   fat   _____

pig   _____   thick   _____

oil   _____   seed   _____

last   _____   Christ   _____

obey   _____   barn   _____

garden   _____   swim   _____

west   _____   oats   _____

☐   I practiced my flashcards today.

LET'S PRACTICE

Draw a line from each balloon to its gingerbread boy.

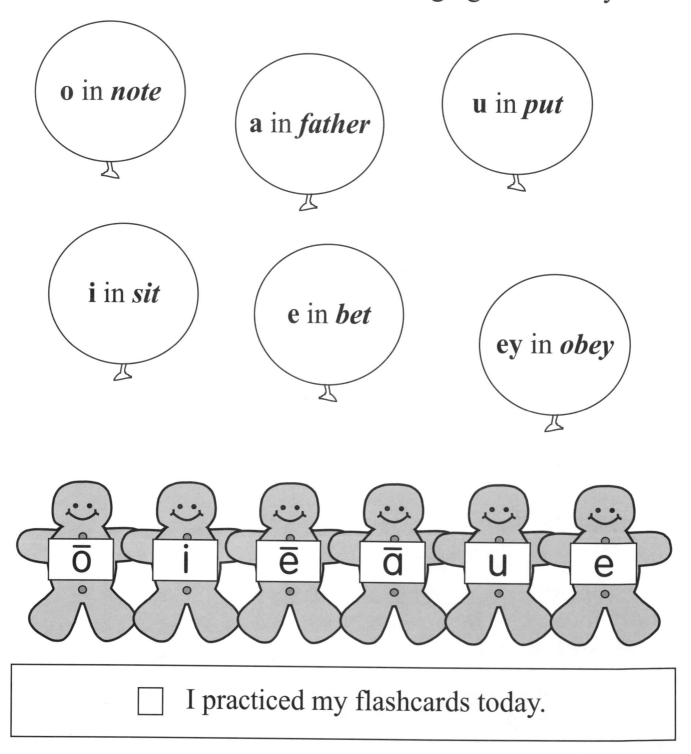

o in *note*

a in *father*

u in *put*

i in *sit*

e in *bet*

ey in *obey*

☐ I practiced my flashcards today.

LET'S PRACTICE

Match the Latin letters with their sounds.

gu   *ps*

bs   *pt*

th   **gu** in *anguish*

bt   **th** in *thick*

ph   **ch** in *character*

ch   *aye*

au   **ph** in *phone*

ae   *ay-oo*

eu   **ow** in *now*

☐ I practiced my flashcards today.

LET'S PRACTICE

Fill in the blanks with the missing sounds and words.

1. Latin **bt** sounds like _____ .

2. Latin **gu** sounds like _____ in _____ .

3. Latin **th** sounds like _____ in _____ .

4. Latin **ph** sounds like _____ in _____ .

5. Latin **bs** sounds like _____ .

6. Latin **ch** sounds like _____ in _____ .

☐ I practiced my flashcards today.

APPENDIX

Latin Alphabet

Capital Letter	Small Letter	Pronunciation	Capital Letter	Small Letter	Pronunciation
Ā	ā	a in *father*	N	n	n in *nut*
A	a	a in *idea*	Ō**	ō**	o in *note*
B	b	b in *boy*	O**	o**	o in *omit*
C	c	c in *cat*	P	p	p in *pit*
D	d	d in *dog*	Q	q	qu in *quit*
Ē	ē	ey in *obey*	R	r	r in *run*
E	e	e in *bet*	S	s	s in *sit*
F	f	f in *fan*	T	t	t in *tag*
G	g	g in *go*	Ū	ū	u in *rule*
H	h	h in *hat*	U	u	u in *put*
Ī	ī	i in *machine*	V	v	w in *way*
I*	i*	i in *sit*	X	x	ks in *socks*
K	k	k in *king*	Ȳ	ȳ	form lips to say "oo" but say "ee" instead (held longer)
L	l	l in *land*	Y	y	form lips to say "oo" but say "ee" instead (held shorter)
M	m	m in *man*	Z	z	dz in *adze*

*When functioning as a consonant, i has the sound of y in *youth*. (See **Special Consonants** below.)
**The ō and the o both have a long o sound, but the ō is held longer.

Special Sounds

Diphthongs

Letters	Pronunciation
ae	*aye*
au	ow in *now*
ei	ei in *neighbor*
eu	*ay-oo*
oe	oy in *joy*
ui	uee in *queen*

Special Consonants

Letters	Pronunciation
bs	*ps*
bt	*pt*
ch	ch in *character*
gu	gu in *anguish*
i	y in *youth*
ph	ph in *phone*
su	su in *suave*
th	th in *thick*

APPENDIX

Flashcard Tips

1. Remember to practice flashcards daily.

2. Do not move ahead in the workbook if your student is struggling for mastery. Review the flashcards every day until your student is confident and ready to learn more.

(front)	(back)
Ā ā	(Start on page 3.) (Level 1) **a** in *father*
A a	(Page 3) (Level 1) **a** in *idea*
B b	(Page 5) (Level 1) **b** in *boy*
C c	(Page 7) (Level 1) **c** in *cat*
D d	(Page 9) (Level 1) **d** in *dog*
Ē ē	(Page 11) (Level 1) **ey** in *obey*

(front)	(back)
E e	(Page 13) (Level 1) **e** in *bet*
F f	(Page 15) (Level 1) **f** in *fan*
G g	(Page 17) (Level 1) **g** in *go*
H h	(Page 19) (Level 1) **h** in *hat*
Ī ī	(Page 21) (Level 1) **i** in *machine*
I i	(Page 23) (Level 1) **i** in *sit*

(front)	(back)
K k	(Page 25) (Level 1) **k** in ***king***
L l	(Page 27) (Level 1) **l** in ***land***
M m	(Page 29) (Level 1) **m** in ***man***
N n	(Page 31) (Level 1) **n** in ***nut***
Ō ō	(Page 33) (Level 1) **o** in ***note***
O o	(Page 35) (Level 1) **o** in ***omit***

(front)	(back)
P p	(Page 37) (Level 1) **p** in ***pit***
Qu qu	(Page 39) (Level 1) **qu** in ***quit***
R r	(Page 41) (Level 1) **r** in ***run***
S s	(Page 43) (Level 1) **s** in ***sit***
T t	(Page 45) (Level 1) **t** in ***tag***
Ū ū	(Page 47) (Level 1) **u** in ***rule***

(front)	(back)
U u	(Page 49) (Level 1) **u** in *put*
V v	(Page 51) (Level 1) **w** in *way*
X x	(Page 53) (Level 1) **ks** in *socks*
Ȳ ȳ	(Page 55) (Level 1) Form your lips to say **oo** but say **ee** instead. (held longer than y)
Y y	(Page 57) (Level 1) Form your lips to say **oo** but say **ee** instead. (held shorter than ȳ)
Z z	(Page 59) (Level 1) **dz** in *adze*

(front)	(back)
ae	(Page 63) (Level 1) *"aye"*
au	(Page 65) (Level 1) **ow** in ***now***
ei	(Page 67) (Level 1) **ei** in ***neighbor***
eu	(Page 69) (Level 1) *"ay-oo"* (in one syllable)
oe	(Page 71) (Level 1) **oy** in ***joy***
ui	(Page 73) (Level 1) **uee** in ***queen***

(front)	(back)
bs	(Page 77) (Level 1) *"ps"*
bt	(Page 79) (Level 1) *"pt"*
ch	(Page 81) (Level 1) **ch** in *character*
gu	(Page 83) (Level 1) **gu** in *anguish*
i	(Page 85) (Level 1) **y** in *youth*
ph	(Page 87) (Level 1) **ph** in *phone*

(front)	(back)
	(Page 89) (Level 1)
su	**su** in ***suave***
	(Page 91) (Level 1)
th	**th** in ***thick***